Nicholas & discover Pordenone

By Max Teia

For you.

*"One needs a town, if only for the pleasure of leaving it.
A town means not being alone, knowing that in the people,
the trees, the soil, there is something of yourself, that even
when you're not there it stays and waits for you."*

The Moon and the Bonfires by Cesare Pavese

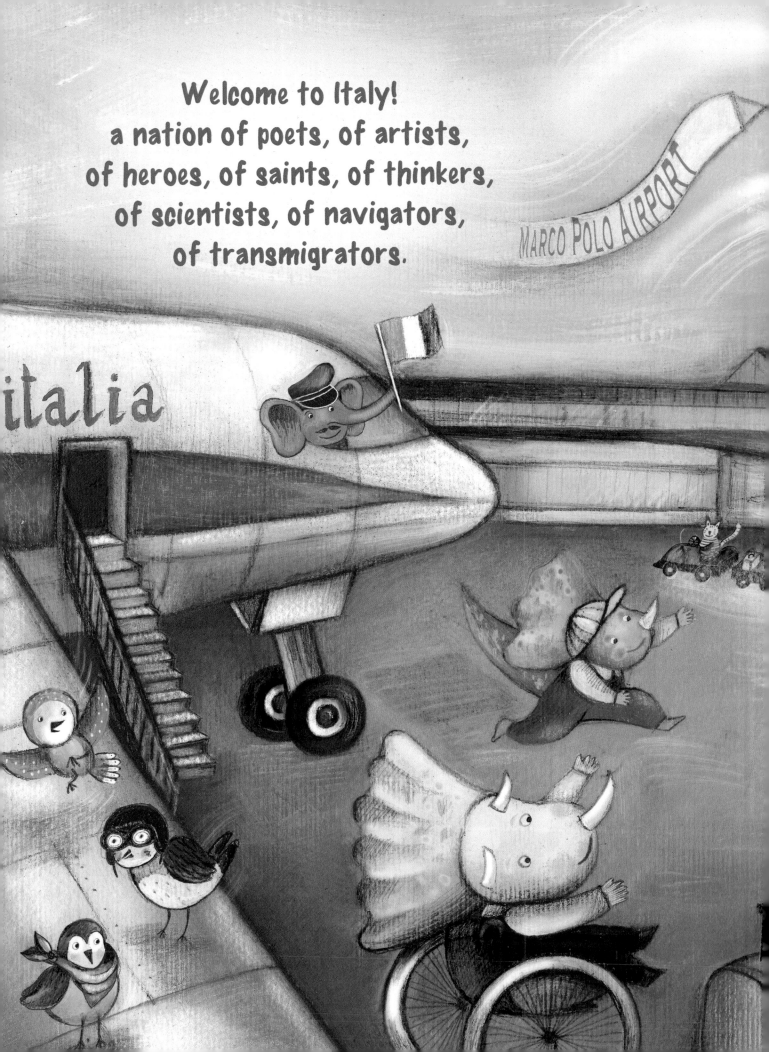

Welcome to Italy!
a nation of poets, of artists,
of heroes, of saints, of thinkers,
of scientists, of navigators,
of transmigrators.

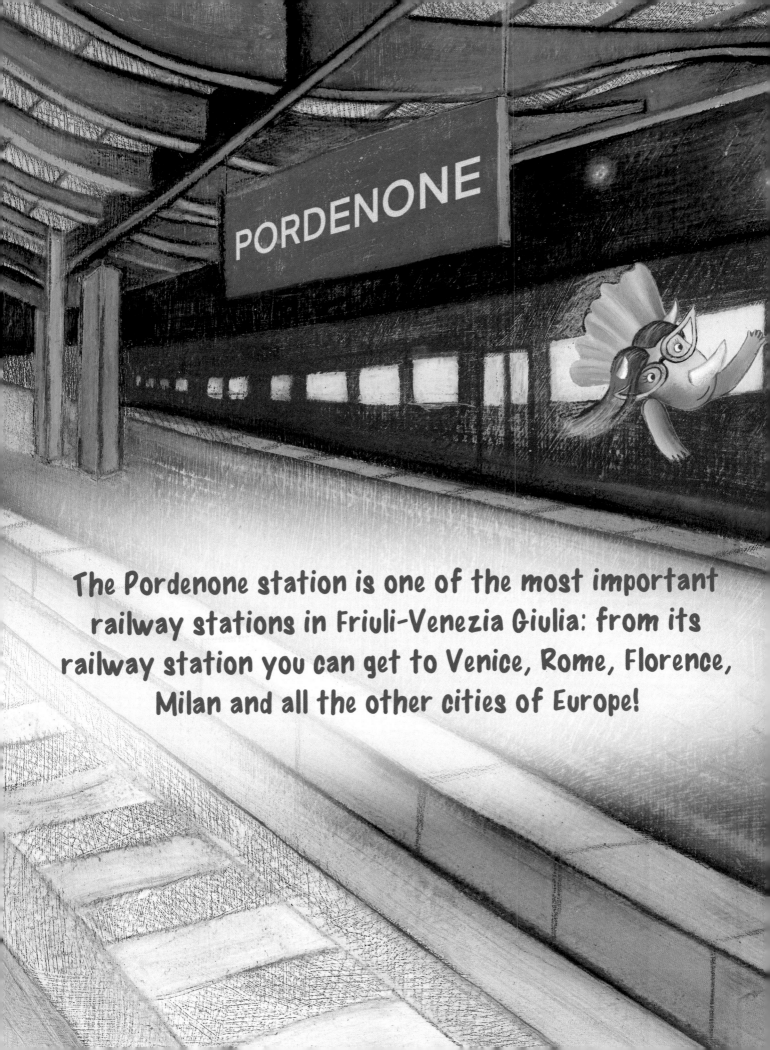

The Pordenone station is one of the most important railway stations in Friuli-Venezia Giulia: from its railway station you can get to Venice, Rome, Florence, Milan and all the other cities of Europe!

Pordenone, Caput Mundi! - said Nonno

Pordenone is a sophisticated city with
a beautifully preserved historic center.
Its arcades, that house ancient cafes,
are among the longest in Europe, but the real charm
of the city are the frescoed noble palaces.
The columns and facades of the buildings are covered
with works of art decorated
with fascinating chromatic shades.

The origin of Pordenone is linked to the existence of the port on the Noncello river. Commercial transit city between the Venetian territories and the Nordic area, thanks to the waterway constituted by the Noncello: all navigable rivers up to the Adriatic sea.

Adam and Eve Bridge: The bridge takes its name from the two statues, popularly called Adam and Eve, but actually representations of Jupiter and Juno.

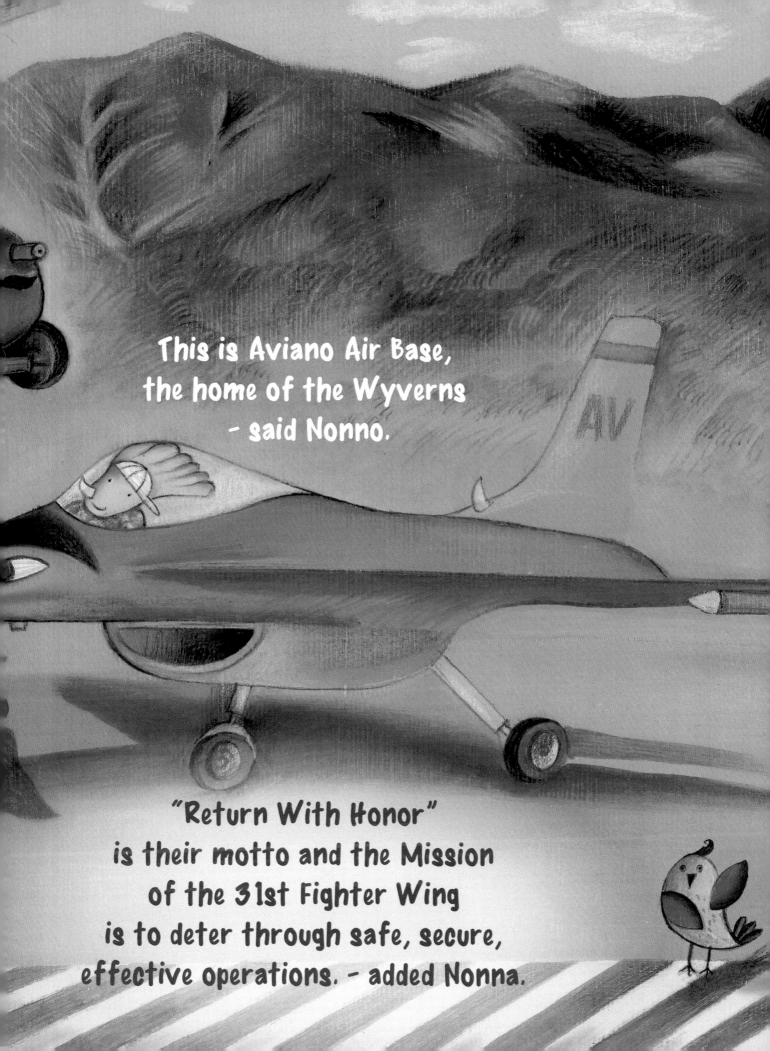

This is Aviano Air Base,
the home of the Wyverns
- said Nonno.

"Return With Honor"
is their motto and the Mission
of the 31st Fighter Wing
is to deter through safe, secure,
effective operations. - added Nonna.

Win the current fight
and be ready to win the next fight!
- cheered together Nicholas and Sofia.

Piancavallo is a ski resort in the Dolomites
at 1,280m (4,199ft) above sea level,
at the foot of Monte Cavallo at 2,251m (7,385ft).

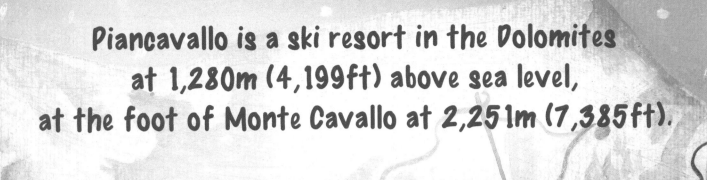

Piancavallo was the first Italian
ski resort with snowmaking facilities.
It has hosted several alpine skiing
events in the World Cup
and the Giro d'Italia cycling race.

MONTE SAUC

MONTE TREMOL

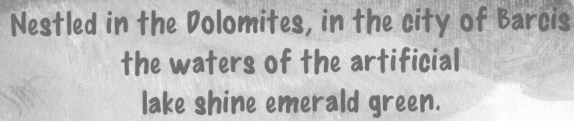

Nestled in the Dolomites, in the city of Barcis
the waters of the artificial
lake shine emerald green.
In this lake you can practice many sports activities,
from sailing to windsurf, underwater sports,
canoeing, fishing and hovercraft.
Even a meteorite was found during the construction
of the Antoi bridge's dam!

Poffabro is an open-air museum in the heart of the Val Colvera.
Its "magic power" is in the spell-like effect of live cut stones and wooden balconies.

The beauty of the village is precisely in the humble reality of stone pillars, staircases, balustrades and arches in perfect harmony with the surrounding nature.

In the cold winter, during Christmas the characteristic silence of this village will leave room for voices and presences who will come to admire the many nativity scenes set up in every corner of the town...

But be careful! In the Mount Raut behind Poffabro, it is said that at night, some witches often gathered to meet the devil...

In mid-September in Valvasone, one of the most beautiful villages in Italy, which also housed Napoleon, it is possible to experience the medieval atmosphere during the historical re-enactment, where thousands of people meet, rushed to admire costumed figures, Knights and ladies, flag-wavers, artisans and alchemists.

Palmanova is a city-fortress preserved in extraordinary conditions. Built in 1593 by the Republic of Venice, is today part of the Unesco Heritage site.

With its plant in the shape of a perfect nine-pointed star, monumental entrance gates and three circles of fortifications from the 16th, 17th and 19th centuries, Palmanova is both a model of an ideal Renaissance city and an example of military architecture.

Inspirational location for a Nobel prize in Literature
winner who called it the Italian Florida
and wrote of it in a memorable book, Lignano Sabbiadoro
"Lignano from the golden sand" is one
of the most successful Italian beaches.

The marina of Lignano
is the largest in Italy
and among the largest in Europe.

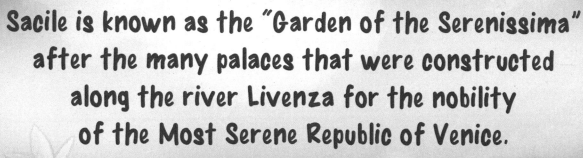

Sacile is known as the "Garden of the Serenissima"
after the many palaces that were constructed
along the river Livenza for the nobility
of the Most Serene Republic of Venice.

In the historic center of Sacile
the palaces have two different entrances:
one from the river and one from the street,
enhancing the harmony and charm of the river city.

The "Famee Furlane" loves to eat around the "Fogolar".
The "Fogolar" signifies the heart or the fireplace
which is the centre of the family life.

Pordenone and its flavors: history has characterized
the cuisine of this land, which has its roots in peasant
traditions, to which are added the contribution of people
and traditions that have also influenced the dishes.

Ordering Information:
For details, contact info@discoveringPN.com.

Print ISBN:978-1-09835-496-1
eBook ISBN:978-1-09835-497-8

Printed in the United States of America.

First Edition